MISSION SURVIVAL:
SAVING EARTH'S ENDANGERED ANIMALS

SAVING THE SHARK

SARAH EASON

CHERITON
CHILDREN'S BOOKS

Published in 2026 by **Cheriton Children's Books**
1 Bank Drive West, Shrewsbury, Shropshire SY3 9DJ, UK

First Edition

Author: Sarah Eason
Designer: Paul Myerscough
Editor: Jane Brooke
Proofreader: Ella Newby
Consultant: David Hawksett, BSc

Picture credits: Cover: Shutterstock/Kaschibo. Inside: pp4-5: Shutterstock/Jsegalexplore, p6: Shutterstock/LuckyStep, p7bl: Shutterstock/Vladimir Wrangel, p7br: Shutterstock/Natia Tsuleiskiri, p7t: Shutterstock/Jeng Bo Yuan, p8: Shutterstock/Martin Rejzek, p11: Shutterstock/Tatiana Belova, p12: Shutterstock/Martin Prochazkacz, p12b: Shutterstock/Wildestanimal, p13b: Shutterstock/Fiona Ayerst, p13c: Shutterstock/Jessica Heim, p13t: Shutterstock/Sergey Uryadnikov, pp14-15: Shutterstock/Fiona Ayerst, pp16-17: Shutterstock/Carlos Grillo, p17b: Shutterstock/Red Fox Studio, p17c: Shutterstock/Red Fox Studio, pp18-19: Shutterstock/Stefan Pircher, p19t: Shutterstock/Mnabeck, p20: Shutterstock/Andre Johnson, p20b: Shutterstock/Jurgal Photographer, p21c: Flickr/Semarnat, p21t: Shutterstock/Animanish, pp22-23: Shutterstock/Fiona Ayerst, p23c: Shutterstock/SeventyFour, p23t: Shutterstock/SeventyFour, pp24-25: Shutterstock/Ethan Daniels, p25: Shutterstock, pp26-27: Shutterstock/Peter Douglas Clark, p27b: Shutterstock/Daniel Majak, p27c: Shutterstock, p27t: Shutterstock/The Law of Adventures, pp28-29: Shutterstock/Jsegalexplore, p28b: Shutterstock/Ksenia Shu, p29c: Shutterstock/Travelview, p29t: Shutterstock/Travelview, pp30-31: Shutterstock/Vlad61, p31b: Shutterstock/Poggensee, p32b: Shutterstock/Tunatura, p32t: Shutterstock/Frantisekhojdysz, p33c: Shutterstock/Captain Gillespie, p33t: Shutterstock/Arunee Rodloy, pp34-35: Shutterstock/Olesia Bilkei, p35b: Shutterstock/Wavebreakmedia, p35c: Shutterstock/Monkey Business Images, p35t: Shutterstock/Monkey Business Images, pp36-37: Shutterstock/ChameleonsEye, p36b: Shutterstock/Rafeed Hussain, p38b: Shutterstock/VI Photo, p38t: Shutterstock/Rich Carey, p39b: Shutterstock/Chonlasub Woravichan, p39t: Shutterstock/Heine Jensen, pp40-41: Shutterstock, p41b: Shutterstock/LightField Studios, p41c: Shutterstock/LightField Studios, p42: Shutterstock, p43: Shutterstock/Mgarcia Creative, p44: Shutterstock/James Kirkikis, p45: Shutterstock/Yann Hubert.

Printed in China

Publisher's Note: The information in the Kids on a Mission features in this book are suggestions for actions that children can take to help protect endangered animals, based on extensive research by the author and consultant. The email addresses and the children featured in the photographs are for illustrative purposes only.

Please visit our website,
www.cheritonchildrensbooks.com,
to see more of our high-quality books.

CONTENTS

SHARKS IN DANGER

Sharks are incredible animals. These kings of the ocean are feared hunters, and many people are very frightened of sharks. But these creatures face far more threats than humans. In fact, sharks have far more to fear from us than we do from them.

HUMANS ARE A DANGER

In the last 50 years, shark **populations** have decreased by 70 percent due to human activities. Some species of shark, such as the oceanic whitetip shark, have even declined, or gone down in number, by up to 98 percent. The amount of scalloped hammerhead sharks in the world is believed to have decreased by 80 percent. It is estimated that around 100 million sharks are killed every year by people. That is an astonishing number, but many people believe it could be far higher. Sharks are being killed deliberately for their meat, **fins**, and other body parts. They are also killed accidentally when people fish other sea creatures. They are also dying because their **habitats** are being harmed due to human activity.

LOST FOREVER

Some **species** of shark are at risk of dying out. They are described as **critically endangered** and at risk of **extinction**. More than 30 percent of shark species are also under great threat. **Conservationists** are warning us that if we do not do more to save these threatened sharks, they may soon be gone forever.

"Sharks have been swimming in the ocean for more than 400 million years... They deserve our respect and protection."

Thomas Peschak, **marine** photographer and conservationist

HELP THE SHARK!

But there is still hope for sharks, and it is not too late to save them. People everywhere have learned about sharks and their need for protection. And they are making it their mission to help these amazing animals survive. In this book, we'll learn about the shark and why it is in danger. We'll discover what people are doing to help sharks and how they have built a career in **conservation**. We'll find out how kids on a mission are saving the shark, and what you can do to help. And we'll learn how you could make a career in conservation your mission. Feeling mission-ready? Then read on!

▲ If we lose these magnificent animals, we'll lose some of our planet's most awe-inspiring creatures.

The International Union for Conservation of Nature (IUCN) keeps a record of the world's species and how at risk of extinction they are. It is called the **Red List.**

There are more than **46,000** animal species on the List.

Some species of sharks are among the most **endangered.**

CHAPTER ONE

MEET THE SHARK

Sharks come in many shapes and sizes. Some are huge killing machines, such as the great white shark, which can grow up to 23 feet long (7 m) and weigh between 1,500–4,400 pounds (680–2,000 kg). Others, like the whale shark, are gentle giants, growing to 40–60 feet (12–18 m) long. Some sharks are tiny, such as the spined pygmy shark, which is just 11 inches (28 cm) long.

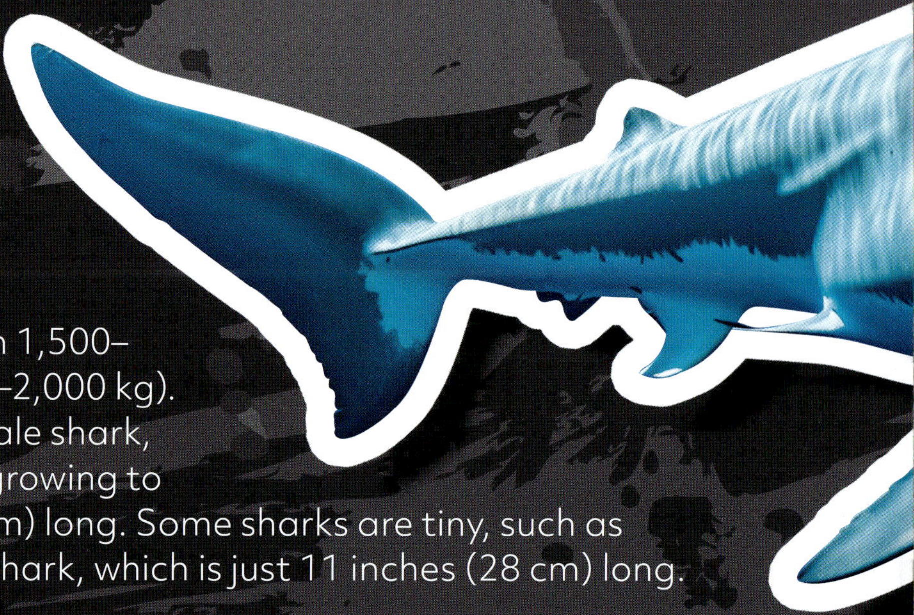

SKELETONS AND SKIN

Although sharks are a type of fish, they are quite different in some ways. For example, most fish have skeletons made of bones, but sharks have skeletons made of material that can easily bend. It is called cartilage. And while most fish have **scales**, sharks have a skin that is very rough to the touch.

TIP TO TOE

The majority of sharks have very powerful and muscular bodies. A shark's body is designed for speed, and many sharks can swim at up to 20 miles per hour (32 kph). They also have upturned tails and pointed fins, and most are armed with deadly, razor-sharp teeth that grip onto **prey** and tear through flesh. Sharks would not be successful hunters without their amazing **senses**. These animals can hear and smell their prey from far away. They even have a special sense, which gives them the ability to detect electrical signals given out by prey.

MANY DIFFERENT COLORS

Sharks generally have a gray-colored skin, but some sharks can be cream, yellow, or brown. Others are blue or almost black. Sharks that are not gray in color often have some patterning, such as spots or stripes.

GREAT HUNTERS AND GENTLE GIANTS

Some sharks are deadly hunters that attack prey with speed, delivering killer bites. However, not all sharks are fierce predators. For example, whale sharks and basking sharks feed only on **plankton** and small sea animals. They have huge mouths that take in large amounts of seawater. As the water is pushed through the sharks' special **gills**, tiny animals become trapped within them.

In a Group

Scientists group animals to help classify, or order, them. Sharks belong to a group of animals called *Chondrichthyes*, which are fish that have cartilage skeletons. Other members of this group include rays, skates, and chimaeras.

WHERE SHARKS LIVE

Sharks have been around for hundreds of millions of years —they were even swimming in Earth's oceans before the dinosaurs appeared. Sharks are amazingly **adaptable** animals that are found in almost all marine environments in the world.

FROM COAST TO DEEP WATER

Sharks swim in coastal waters around the world, visiting bays, **estuaries**, and coral reefs. Sharks that particularly like these areas include great white sharks, tiger sharks, and hammerhead sharks. Further out to sea, some sharks hunt and live in the open ocean. They include oceanic whitetip sharks, blue sharks, and mako sharks. Some sharks are deep-sea survivors, living in deep ocean trenches and dark and murky waters far below the ocean surface. They include goblin sharks, frilled sharks, and dogfish.

COLD-WATER SHARKS

Some sharks swim in the icy-cold waters of the Arctic and Antarctic Oceans. They include Greenland sharks, which are believed to live for an incredibly long time (at least 250 years and possibly more than 500 years!). They have a slow **metabolism** that helps them survive in the freezing conditions where they live.

▼ Oceanic whitetip sharks are long-distance swimmers that live far out at sea, where they face threats from fishing ships. The sharks are often caught in nets along with other fish.

LONG-DISTANCE SWIMMERS

Some species of shark travel huge distances to search for food or **breed**. They include:

- great white sharks
- whale sharks
- tiger sharks
- hammerhead sharks
- blue sharks
- mako sharks
- basking sharks

DANGERS OF TRAVEL

When sharks travel long distances, it puts them at risk. Conservation laws are different in one country to the next, so when traveling sharks cross boundaries and enter another country's **territory** at sea, they can be at risk from fishing and other threats. Some parts of Earth's oceans do not belong to any country and are called high seas. When sharks swim in these areas, they do not have any protection from the law and can be easily hunted and killed.

INTO THE RIVERS

Not all sharks live only in the ocean. Some unusual species of shark can live in both salt water and fresh water. They are bull sharks. These hardy and adaptable sharks swim in both oceans and rivers. Unlike most other types of sharks, they can survive in fresh water.

▼ Sharks are found in oceans all over the world. Bull sharks are found in rivers too.

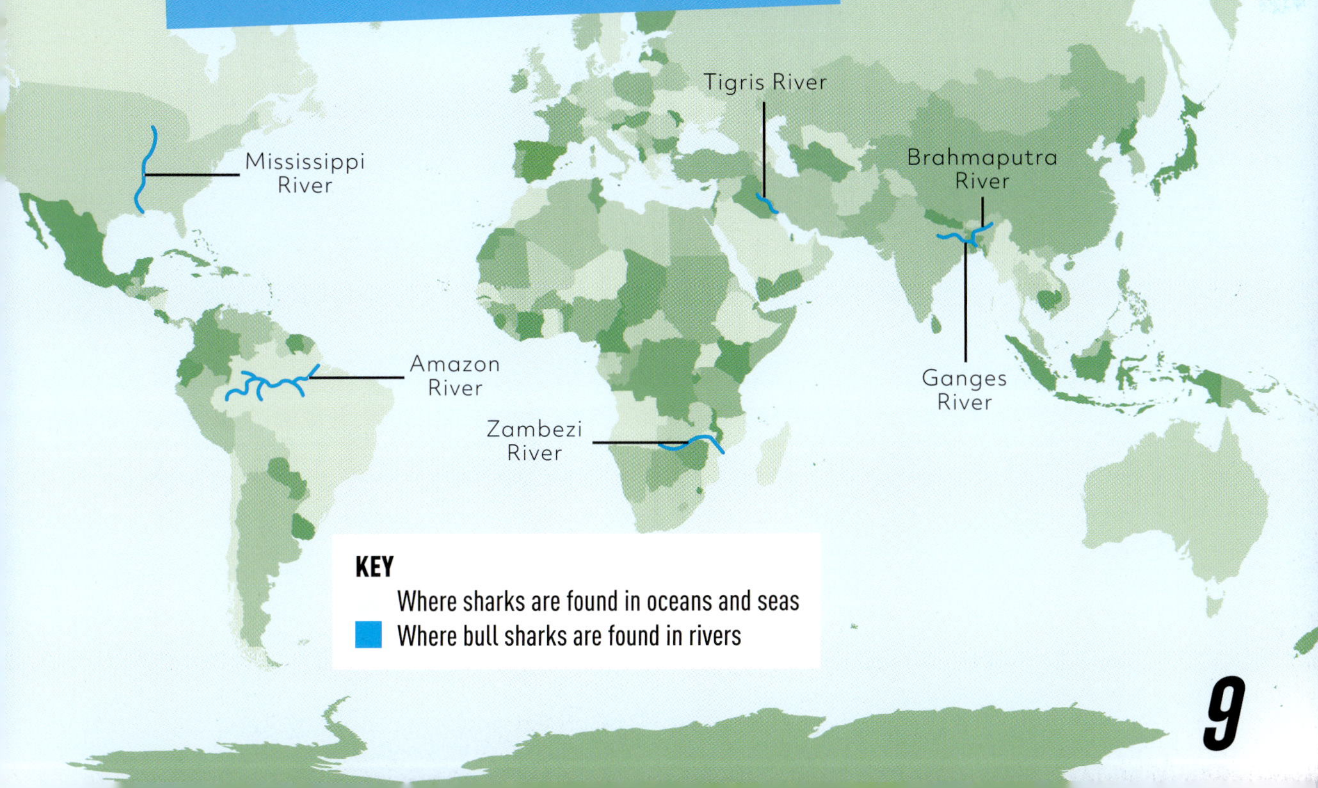

WHY SHOULD WE HELP THE SHARK?

Sharks are incredibly important to the many **environments** in which they live. Sharks are apex predators. That means they are at the top of their food chain. Sharks hunt other animals in the food chain and have only a few natural predators, including orcas, sperm whales, and other sharks.

SHARK CONTROL

Sharks help control their ecosystem and keep ocean and sea life in balance. That is because they hunt animals within it that would otherwise become too great in number. Some of the animals that sharks hunt are herbivores. These are plant-eating animals. If they become too numerous, they could eat too many of the ocean and sea plants they feed on. These plants would then die out. That would leave no food for the herbivores. Then, they too would die out. Sharks also help maintain healthy populations of prey animals. That is because they target sick, injured, or weak animals for food. By removing them, sharks help prevent the spread of disease and keep the overall population of prey animals healthy.

HABITAT PROTECTOR

Sharks also help protect precious seagrass areas. Seagrass meadows are homes and feeding grounds for many important animals including sea turtles, dugongs, and manatees. Sharks feed on sea turtles, and will kill and eat sick or injured dugongs and manatees. By controlling the populations of these animals, sharks help stop seagrass meadows becoming **overgrazed**.

▼ This leopard shark is swimming near a reef populated with many fish. Without sharks, populations of fish and other animals that sharks feed on would grow out of control and the ecosystem would be damaged.

What Is an Ecosystem?

An ecosystem is a group of natural parts that all work together for a purpose. Ecosystems include nonliving things such as water, sunshine, and air. These are called abiotic factors. Ecosystems also include living things such as plants and animals. These are called biotic factors. The living things in an ecosystem depend on the abiotic factors in the ecosystem to survive. Every part of the ecosystem has an important part to play. A healthy ecosystem has many different plants and animals living together. If any part of that ecosystem changes or is damaged, the other parts are affected, too.

TOP OF THE FOOD CHAIN

Most sharks are built to hunt. They are one of nature's most powerful and successful predators. Almost everything about a shark makes it a super killer.

SMELLING AND HEARING

A shark attack can begin when the killer's prey is still very far away. Sounds travel fast in water, so the shark may hear the animal even before it smells it. As the prey moves, the shark listens for the very low sounds it makes, and follows them.

MADE FOR SPEED

A shark streaks through the water at great speed. It is streamlined, like many fish, and moves its tail from side to side to propel itself forward. The shark's long, strong body contains powerful muscles that make the tail lash to move the shark through the water.

TWIST AND TURN

A shark's fins also help it twist and turn. They allow the shark to get into a good position above its prey before attacking. A shark has a large fin in the middle of its back, called the dorsal fin, and may also have smaller fins near its tail. The fins allow it to steer and to stay level in the water. Sharks often circle their food, swimming around and around it, before they attack. When they do attack, they usually do so from beneath. As the shark closes in, it uses its fins to maneuver around its prey, then it slams into it! The shark moves so quickly, it usually takes its prey by surprise.

KILLER JAWS

With larger prey, the shark clamps its jaws around part of the animal's body and rips off a mouthful of flesh. It swallows smaller fish whole! Large tiger sharks can even crush the tough shells of sea turtles. A shark has up to 3,000 razor-sharp teeth, which are arranged in its mouth in several rows.

CAMOUFLAGED KILLER

Sharks can often get close to their prey without being spotted because most sharks are **camouflaged**. Tiger sharks, for example, have a light-colored belly, so they blend with the sky when they are seen from below. Their dark back, however, makes them difficult to see from above.

PEOPLE ON A MISSION

Many people are concerned about what is happening to sharks and are making it their mission to help save them. They have found careers in marine conservation as a way to protect sharks. These are some examples of the ways in which people are working to protect sharks around the world.

PEOPLE ON THE GROUND

Protecting the shark's habitat and monitoring its numbers are very important. There are a number of vital jobs in which people carry out work to protect shark homes and maintain their numbers. Wildlife conservationists check shark populations and the health of the places where they swim. Fishery managers make sure sustainable fishing practices are put in place to help protect shark populations. Environmental educators raise awareness about sharks and their important role in their ecosystems.

PEOPLE IN OFFICES

Conservation organizations are also working with the governments of countries that control waters where sharks live. Together, they are creating systems that protect the sharks and their habitats. There are also charities in which people work hard to help raise money to save sharks. Communications and public relations experts help organizations raise awareness about sharks.

PEOPLE IN THE LAB

Scientists are helping sharks too. **Marine biologists** and research technicians study sharks to find out more about them, and how we can help them. Marine data analysts collect information from shark research and monitoring programs to better understand what is happening to populations of sharks around the world.

MAKE IT YOUR MISSION

You could help sharks and other endangered animals by taking action and planning a career in conservation. Here's how:

1. In this book, you'll discover what actions kids on a mission can take to help sharks. Use them to inspire your own actions to help protect sharks.
2. You'll also discover some of the careers people on a mission have in shark conservation. As you read about each one, consider if that career in conservation might suit you.
3. At the end of this book, you'll find a guide on how to build a career in conservation. Check it out to discover how you can make saving animals your life mission.

▼ Ryan Johnson is a shark biologist. He is also a conservationist who is helping educate people about sharks. Ryan has made many films and television documentaries about sharks, and has spent more than 20 years studying these amazing animals to learn more about them.

PEOPLE EVERYWHERE

And ordinary people everywhere, including kids just like you, are raising money to help sharks and educate others about the threats they face. They are finding creative ways to raise awareness about sharks and why they are in danger. They are joining organizations that help protect sharks. They are changing their lifestyle practices to help protect the shark and other marine animals. They want a world in which sharks are still around for their children to see.

CHAPTER TWO

HOMES UNDER THREAT

Sharks need healthy **habitats** in which they can hunt, feed, and reproduce, or have young. Unfortunately, human activities are making shark habitats dangerous places to live.

TAKING OVER SHARK HOMES

As the human population grows, more and more buildings are constructed along coastlines, harming important shark habitats. They include **mangrove** forests, seagrass meadows, and coral reefs. When people clear and build on land near these coastal places, habitats where the animals can hunt and in which baby sharks can shelter and develop are reduced.

POLLUTED WATERS

Today, plastic **pollution** is a huge problem for all marine animals, including the shark. Our garbage makes its way into rivers and oceans, where it becomes a hazard for the animals that live there. Sharks may eat plastic waste, which is harmful to them. They can also become entangled in plastic debris, which often kills them. Chemical pollution from farming and industrial activities such as manufacturing also enters coastal waters. It pollutes the water, which harms the habitat and endangers the health of sharks. And when oil spills take place at sea, that can be devastating to sharks. The oil poisons the water, harming both the sharks and their prey.

HURTING HABITATS

The building of physical barriers in coastal areas, such as dams and harbors, breaks up shark habitats and makes it difficult for the animals to survive in those places. The traffic that then passes through those areas, from boats to ships, also disturbs wildlife. That makes it difficult for sharks to hunt and feed in the areas. It also reduces the sharks' ability to breed. Sharks are even hit by passing traffic, such as ships, and killed.

▲ Seagrass meadows are important habitats for sharks such as this bull shark. Unfortunately, these areas are being damaged by many activities including pollution and fishing.

Kids on a Mission

@kelly_sharksurvival_22

I try and raise awareness about what amazing animals sharks are at school so that more people will get involved with shark conservation. My class has adopted a shark through Shark Angels.

"Protecting (shark) habitats is ... about **preserving** the health of our oceans."

Sylvia Earle, marine biologist

SPOTLIGHT ON SHARK TOURISM

Some people want to see sharks in real life. They pay to travel on boats to watch sharks in their natural environment. Some people even observe the animals underwater, while protected inside metal cages. These people are part of a growing **tourism** business—shark tourism.

GOOD AND BAD

Shark tourism can have both a positive and negative effect on sharks. When carried out responsibly, shark tourism can help the efforts of conservationists. Shark tourists get to see sharks in their natural environment, discover that these creatures are not uncontrollable killers, but instead a vital part of their ecosystem. That all helps people develop a respect for sharks and a desire to protect them. However, when shark tourism is not properly controlled it can lead to problems. Too many tourists on boats can disturb shark behavior. It disrupts their usual feeding patterns and can cause the animals stress.

▲ Cage-diving to watch sharks is becoming ever-more popular in many places around the world, including off the coast of South Africa where great white sharks can often be observed.

▲ If humans and sharks come into contact, there is always the chance that injuries to people may occur.

PEOPLE ON A MISSION: TOURISTS SUPPORTING SHARKS

Some **conservationists** and conservation organizations work to ensure that shark tourism is responsible and benefits sharks and local communities. They work with tourism operators, governments, and local people to put together tourist activities that do not harm shark habitats or sharks.

Conservation organizations encourage shark tourism that does not involve feeding sharks or disturbing their natural habitats. They promote activities that include shark-watching, snorkeling, and diving, while maintaining a safe distance from the sharks. That allows the sharks to remain undisturbed and free to behave in a normal way.

Some responsible shark tourism providers include education as part of their activities. They provide guided tours during which tourists learn about shark bodies, conservation issues, and the importance of sharks in marine ecosystems. Sometimes, tourists get the chance to take part in science programs, helping gather information about sharks that contributes to further research. Tourists are also given opportunities to take incredible photographs or films of sharks in their natural environments. Those images may then too be used for research or to help raise awareness of sharks in conservation missions.

SHARK FEEDING

In some parts of the world, feeding sharks by hand is a tourist activity. People pay to be taken by boat to places in which sharks are known to swim. They then dive in those waters, and may be allowed to feed fish and pieces of meat to sharks. While this can be an exciting experience for some people, it can lead to problems. Being fed by hand is not part of a shark's usual feeding pattern. Inevitably, accidents occur.

SHARING ITS HOME

A lot of different ocean creatures swim in the same waters in which sharks live. Sadly, many of them are also endangered.

THE SEA TURTLE

Sea turtles, like sharks, are under threat. They are hunted for food, but also face danger from habitat destruction. Beaches on which the animals make nests in which to lay their eggs are often disturbed by people, and sea turtle eggs are also stolen. They are then sold in markets and restaurants, where they are a prized food in some parts of the world. Sea turtles are also harmed by plastic in seas and oceans. When they swallow it, they can choke on the plastic. Like sharks, sea turtles also become entangled in old fishing nets, and drown.

THE MANATEE

These large water-living **mammals** live in coastal waters including bays, **estuaries**, **lagoons**, and mangrove forests. Like the sharks they live alongside, they face threats from damage to their habitat from pollution and construction work, including the building of towns and cities along coastal areas. Dams and harbors built near manatee homes also create problems. Boats moving through these areas often hit manatees, which can injure or kill them. Manatees also become entangled in fishing nets, which can cause deep cuts on their bodies. If they are caught underwater in the nets for too long, and are unable to come to the surface to breathe, they will drown.

THE VAQUITA

The vaquita is a small **porpoise** that lives in the Gulf of California. One of the greatest threats to the animal is the fishing of totoaba, a fish that swims in the same waters as the vaquita. Totoaba has been fished in huge numbers, because its **bladder** is used in Chinese herbal medicine. Although the fishing of totoaba is illegal, it still continues. The Vaquitas get caught in the same nets used to fish totoaba, and drown because they cannot reach the surface to breathe. Vaquita also face other threats to their habitat, including the increasing problem of pollution.

THE ATLANTIC BLUEFIN TUNA

The Atlantic Bluefin Tuna is in danger because it has been overfished. The demand for tuna fish around the world has led to an enormous amount of the tuna being caught, which has greatly reduced the population. An added problem is that the tuna take a long time to reach adulthood, at which point they can reproduce. For that reason, it is very difficult for them to replace their numbers quickly and recover from overfishing. Restrictions on the number of tuna that can be fished has helped their population recover a little.

CHAPTER THREE

UNDER THREAT FROM FISHING

Fishing is one of the biggest threats to sharks. They are caught both on purpose and by accident. Shark fishing greatly reduces shark populations, making it difficult for the animals to maintain their numbers.

THE PROBLEM OF OVERFISHING

Some species of sharks are fished especially for their fins, meat, liver oil, and other body parts. These include tiger, basking, thresher, hammerhead, silky, and mako sharks. In some parts of Asia, shark fins are greatly valued for their use in shark fin soup. The demand for the food drives the demand for shark fishing. When too many are caught, shark numbers drop quickly. That puts their survival at risk. This type of fishing of one species is known as overfishing. Even sharks that are not deliberately hunted are threatened by fishing because they may become caught in nets intended for other fish. They then become **bycatch**.

FISHING SHARKS FOR FUN

People who fish as a hobby or sport are called anglers. Some anglers view fishing sharks as an exciting experience. However, the activity puts sharks under threat. Anglers often target large shark species, which are valued for their size or the fight that they put up when caught on a line. When too many of any one type of shark are caught, the entire species can be threatened.

"Shark finning is a cruel and wasteful practice that kills millions of sharks each year. It's time to end this ***inhumane*** trade."

Oceana

Kids on a Mission

@joe_sharkfan_oceans1

My class watched a show about shark fishing at school. No shark should be hunted like that. After watching that show, we researched how to help sharks. We've now joined a shark protection organization.

▲ Even if released, sharks like this mako often die from injuries caused during fishing.

AGAINST THE LAW

The illegal wildlife trade is the illegal trade of wild plants and animals. The business is worth billions of dollars worldwide. Some estimates put the value of the business at between $50 and $150 billion a year. Like many other marine animals, sharks make up part of that business and are victims of the trade. The illegal selling of shark fins and other body parts is an enormous threat to sharks and their survival.

SPOTLIGHT ON **SHARK FINNING**

Shark finning involves catching sharks, removing their fins, then putting the sharks back into the ocean afterward. The sharks are hauled onto a ship deck during the process and their fins are removed with a knife. They are then pushed or thrown back into the water. The sharks are often still alive when they are released, but cannot survive without their fins and later die.

A CRUEL PRACTICE

Shark finning is considered to be cruel and **inhumane**. It also causes huge problems to shark populations and marine ecosystems. Without fins, sharks can't swim. They often starve, suffocate, or are eaten by other animals. Shark finning is banned in many countries, but in other areas it still continues. That is because the market for shark fins in some parts of the world is very high and the income fishermen make from selling shark fins is greater than it is in other areas of fishing.

▲ This bull shark's fins were cut off. Without them, it couldn't survive.

PEOPLE ON A MISSION: PATROL AND EDUCATE

Fishery management specialists work to stop shark finning and encourage sustainable shark fishing practices. They work with people in government to make policies that try and stop shark finning. They help set fishing limits and create plans to protect sharks. They may ban the types of fishing gear that are used in certain types of shark fishing. They also patrol areas in which there are concerns that illegal shark fishing is taking place. In those areas, they will inspect fishing boats to make sure that shark finning is not happening and ensure that sharks are fished only with their fins attached.

The specialists work with local fishermen and fishing communities to try to develop partnerships to encourage sustainable shark fishing. They organize workshops, training sessions, and outreach programs that educate fishermen about the damage to the environment that shark finning causes. They also provide information about other ways of fishing or earning an income that are available, and that are not harmful to sharks. They may offer money in the form of grants to fishermen to help boost their income in exchange for not taking part in illegal shark fishing.

The specialists talk to local people about ways to stop shark finning, and take on board their ideas. Local fishermen are encouraged to monitor and report any cases of shark finning. They are also shown how to handle sharks and release them so that they stand the best chance of survival if they are captured accidentally.

▲ In some parts of the world, including Southeast Asia, fishing for sharks is a local livelihood. This fisherman has caught sharks off the coast of India. Conservationists work with other fishermen to encourage them to find sustainable fishing practices.

BABY SHARKS

Sharks reproduce in a number of ways. In most species, a female produces eggs that **hatch** inside her body. The embryos, or developing babies, then grow inside special cases called "mermaid's purses." When the babies are fully grown, the mother then gives birth to them. Some other types of shark grow their babies inside their body, but not within cases. The embryos develop inside the mother's **uterus**, and she then gives birth to them.

CARRYING BABIES

Sharks can be pregnant for just several months or for more than a year, depending on their species. Nurse sharks are pregnant for just five to six months, for example. Some female sharks are pregnant for a very long time. Tiger sharks are pregnant for up to 16 months, and great white sharks carry their babies for up to 18 months. Spiny dogfish can be pregnant for up to 24 months. Basking sharks are pregnant for even longer—perhaps up to 4 years.

LAYING EGGS

In a few species of shark, the female shark lays eggs. She deposits the mermaid's purses onto the seabed or attaches them to structures such as rocks or seaweed. The embryos then develop outside the mother's body, and hatch from the purses as fully formed baby sharks.

IN DANGER

Once they have hatched or are born, baby sharks are immediately in danger. The little fish are an easy meal for larger fish and marine mammals. They are also eaten by other sharks. Baby sharks spend much of their time hiding from predators, until they are large enough to avoid being easy prey. They often hide in shallow coastal waters, mangrove forests, and coral reefs.

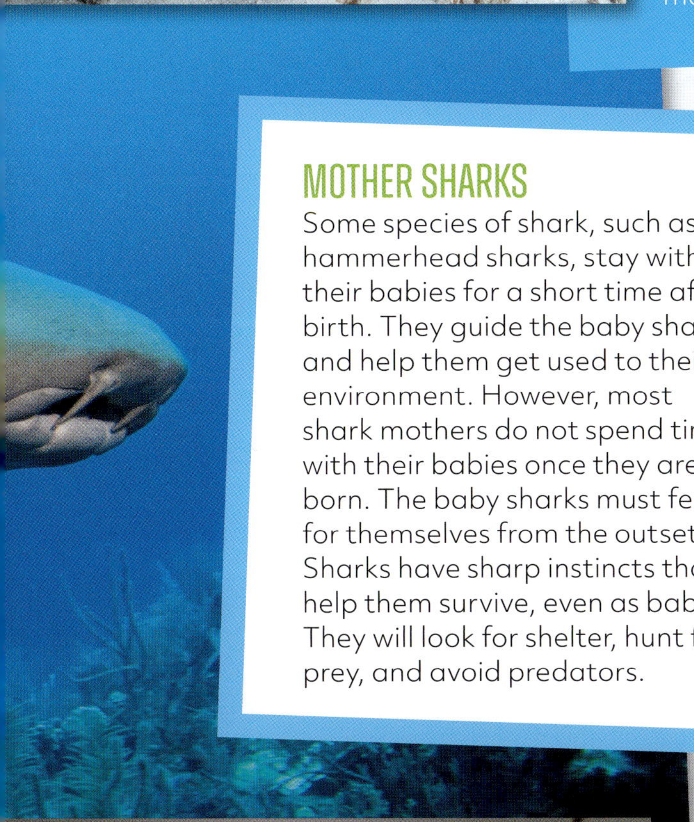

MOTHER SHARKS

Some species of shark, such as hammerhead sharks, stay with their babies for a short time after birth. They guide the baby sharks and help them get used to their environment. However, most shark mothers do not spend time with their babies once they are born. The baby sharks must fend for themselves from the outset. Sharks have sharp instincts that help them survive, even as babies. They will look for shelter, hunt for prey, and avoid predators.

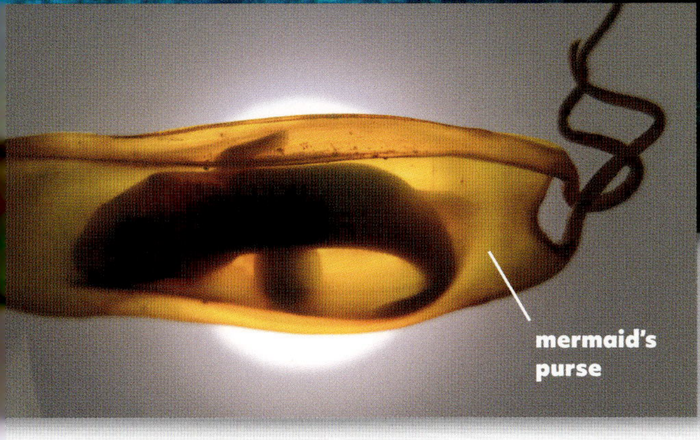

BABIES EATING BABIES!

Life can be dangerous for baby sharks even inside the uterus. In some species of shark, one baby will eat the other baby sharks in the uterus! The first baby shark to hatch from its egg eats its brothers or sisters to help it grow and survive.

CHAPTER FOUR

CLIMATE CHANGE THREATS

Our planet is getting warmer and experiencing more extreme weather patterns. **Climate change** is having an effect on all plants and animals on Earth. Sharks are one of the many species that are suffering because of Earth's changing climate.

WHAT IS CLIMATE CHANGE?

Climate change is a change in temperature or weather in an area over a long period of time. Climate change has always happened slowly throughout Earth's history, due to natural factors such as changes in the sun and **geological** activity. However, the climate change we are experiencing today is largely caused by human activities. These include burning **fossil fuels**, which releases gases into Earth's **atmosphere**. These gases circle the planet, causing it to heat up.

Hurricanes are powerful storms that damage shark habitats. These violent storms are increasing due to climate change. ▶

"Sharks are the guardians of the ocean, but climate change is putting their future at risk. We must act now to protect sharks and the ecosystems they call home."

Ocean Conservancy

Kids on a Mission

@kyle_planetlove_101

Climate change is a big worry. Everyone needs to do what they can to help reduce how we are harming our planet. I've started cycling to school to try and stop how many car journeys we make, and I recycle as much as I can.

◀ Warming ocean waters are a significant threat to all sharks, including the hammerhead shark.

CHANGING OCEANS

Climate change is causing ocean temperatures to rise, which can disrupt the numbers and distribution of prey animals that sharks rely on. If prey species move away to cooler water due to rising ocean temperatures, sharks are left with nothing to eat. Climate change is also damaging shark habitats such as coral reefs, mangrove forest, and seagrass meadows. These areas are important places in which sharks shelter, breed, and hunt and feed. The change in climate is also altering ocean currents. Currents are powerful, often fast-moving flows of water in Earth's oceans. Many sharks rely on ocean currents to carry their food toward them. When the currents change, sharks' food can be reduced.

SPOTLIGHT ON CORAL REEFS

Coral reefs are underwater structures that are homes to many species of sharks, and they too are at threat because of climate change. Coral reefs are made up of animals called polyps. Coral polyps share food with a tiny **algae** that lives among them. Like plants, the algae produce food using energy from sunlight. The problem is they cannot do that in water that is too warm.

Climate change is causing our seas and oceans ▶ to warm up. When the water gets too warm, the algae inside coral die or leave. Without algae, coral cannot get food and starts to die.

DYING CORAL REEFS

Oceans absorb, or take in, **carbon dioxide (CO2)**. This gas in Earth's atmosphere is contributing to climate change. Too much CO2 in the atmosphere changes the chemical makeup of Earth's oceans. It makes them more acidic, which means they have more acid. Acid in the ocean makes it hard for corals to grow. Their skeletons become weak, and they break more easily in storms. Coral reefs are getting weaker and weaker. When storms occur, the reefs struggle to survive them and pieces of coral are easily broken off.

PEOPLE ON A MISSION: GROWING NEW CORAL

Conservationists are working hard to find out more about how climate change is affecting our coral reefs. Scientists called coral reef ecologists focus on studying how coral reef ecosystems work. They observe how coral, sharks and other fish, sea turtles, and many other marine animals operate on coral reefs and behave with each other. They study the health of coral and learn more about how environmental impacts such as climate change affect these important structures.

Other conservationists specialize in **restoring** coral reefs. They work to repair areas of reef that have been damaged and try to restore them to health. They do that with coral gardening. It involves taking sections of healthy coral from reefs and transporting them to coral nurseries. These are protected areas in which coral can safely and healthily grow. Coral nurseries may be floating rafts, underwater tables, or frames in the water that provide a safe and stable place in which coral can grow.

The transported coral is attached to the nursery. Staff check the health and growth of the coral. Pieces are carefully cut off and then reattached to other areas of the nursery. They then too grow into new areas of coral. Once the coral has reached a suitable size, it is transported to damaged reefs and attached to them. The coral is then monitored to make sure it remains healthy in its new home.

◀ Coral is grown in nurseries like this one, then removed and reattached to coral reefs that are at threat.

SHARKS NEED CORAL REEFS

Coral reefs are important places for sharks. They provide them with food and a place to shelter and hide. And sharks are equally important to coral reefs.

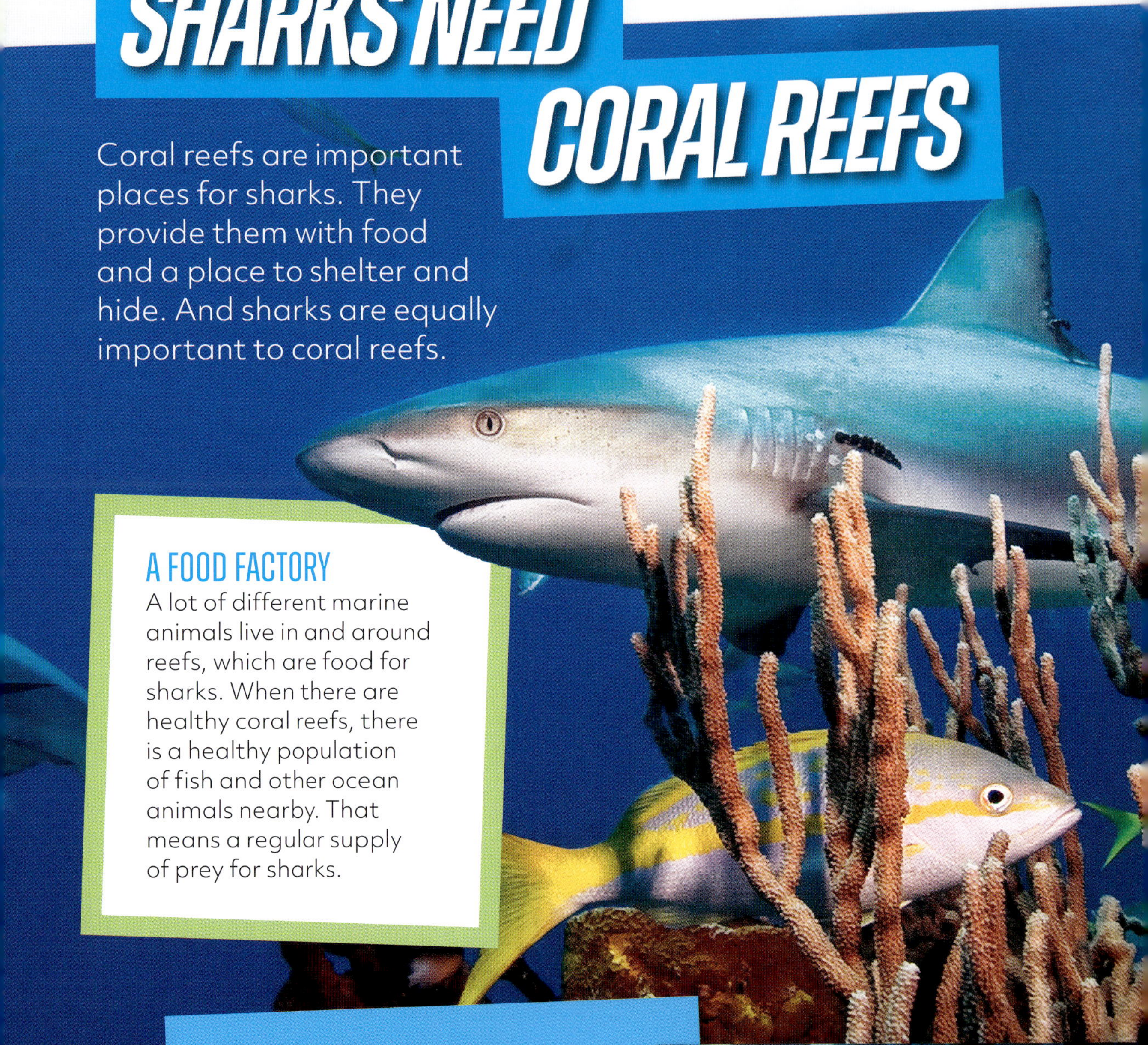

A FOOD FACTORY

A lot of different marine animals live in and around reefs, which are food for sharks. When there are healthy coral reefs, there is a healthy population of fish and other ocean animals nearby. That means a regular supply of prey for sharks.

A PLACE TO HIDE AND HUNT

Coral reefs provide sharks with plenty of places to shelter and hide. Sharks use the reefs as resting places. Within their nooks, crannies, and caves, sharks can rest during the day, safe from other predators. They then come out at night to hunt their prey.

HOMES TO BABIES

Reefs are also places where sharks give birth to baby sharks, or lay their eggs. When shark babies are born or hatch, the reefs are a safe place for the sharks to grow. In the reef are plenty of hiding places for tiny sharks, which bigger predators cannot reach. Coral reefs have plenty of food for baby sharks, and they feed in and around the reef until they are large enough to venture farther afield.

KEEPING REEFS HEALTHY

Sharks are at the top of their food chain. In a food chain, there are producers, primary consumers, and secondary consumers. Producers are plants that provide food for plant-eating animals, which are primary consumers. Plant-eating animals provide food for meat-eating animals—the secondary consumers. Sharks are secondary consumers. Sharks help keep coral reefs healthy because they stop primary consumers growing too great in number. If they did so, they would eat too many of the marine plants that grow on and around coral reefs, which would threaten the reef and its ecosystem.

CHAPTER FIVE

OTHER SHARK CHALLENGES

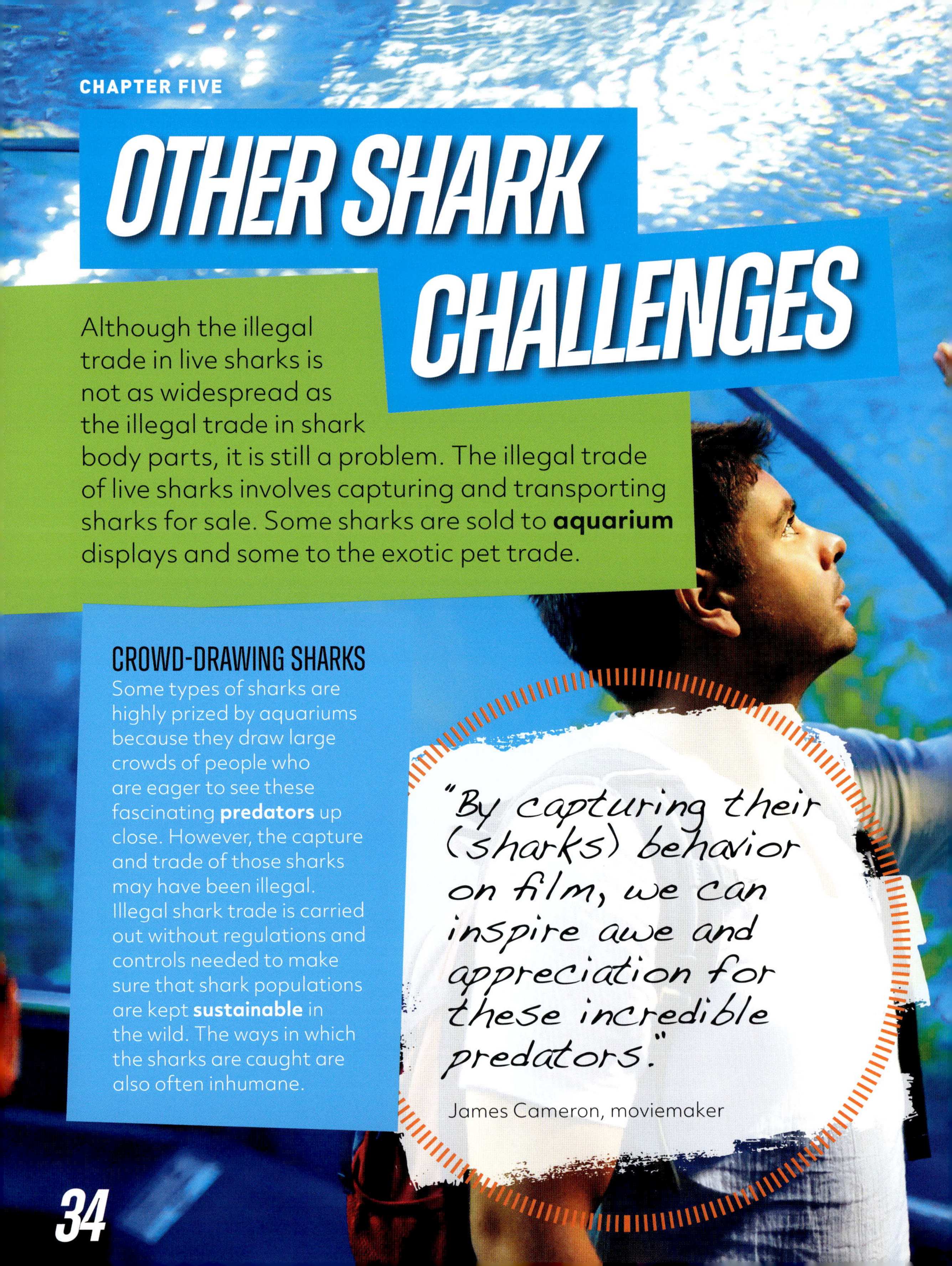

Although the illegal trade in live sharks is not as widespread as the illegal trade in shark body parts, it is still a problem. The illegal trade of live sharks involves capturing and transporting sharks for sale. Some sharks are sold to **aquarium** displays and some to the exotic pet trade.

CROWD-DRAWING SHARKS

Some types of sharks are highly prized by aquariums because they draw large crowds of people who are eager to see these fascinating **predators** up close. However, the capture and trade of those sharks may have been illegal. Illegal shark trade is carried out without regulations and controls needed to make sure that shark populations are kept **sustainable** in the wild. The ways in which the sharks are caught are also often inhumane.

"By capturing their (sharks) behavior on film, we can inspire awe and appreciation for these incredible predators."

James Cameron, moviemaker

Shark aquariums are ▶ places in which people can observe sharks safely, but regulations about how sharks are caught and transported for aquariums are very important.

Kids on a Mission

@julia_shark_action101

With the help of my teacher, I wrote a letter to our county commissioner about the illegal wildlife trade and explained how sharks are being harmed. I asked her to help raise awareness in government about the problem.

▼ Sharks attract crowds of fascinated observers.

SHARKS AS PETS

Sharks are fascinating animals, and some people even want a shark as a pet. Some smaller species of sharks are kept at home by people in aquariums or large tanks. The demand for these highly exotic pets is creating a widespread illegal trade in sharks. That is damaging shark populations in their natural habitat. Sharks are wild animals and they do not belong in a tank in a person's home.

SHARKS FOR RESEARCH

Some live sharks are captured and sold for research. They may be sold to places that want to study sharks, put them in public exhibitions, or run educational programs about them. While research and educational institutions may be legal and their aims are good, the way in which the sharks are captured and handled may not always be so responsible. Unfortunately, the illegal trade of sharks may occur even in areas of research.

SPOTLIGHT ON CAPTIVITY

Although capturing sharks can be harmful to their survival as a species, there are some good reasons why keeping sharks in captivity can help protect the animals in the wild. By keeping sharks and studying them, we can learn more about these mysterious creatures. And the more we know about sharks, the better we can help them in their natural habitat.

SHARKS ARE NOT THE ENEMY

Well-run aquariums and marine parks offer people in the general public a chance to see sharks up-close. Seeing sharks can help people learn more about the animals, their behavior, and why they are so important to their ecosystems. Sharks have had a bad reputation for many years. If people can learn to have a greater understanding and respect for these animals, they'll be more likely to support programs and actions that try and help the shark.

▼ Scientists study shark bodies in research centers and monitor their growth.

▲ In Shark Bay, off the coast of Australia, researchers work in one of the world's largest humanmade **lagoons**. In it, sharks swim freely. The sharks have a safe environment and the scientists who work in the Bay can study them.

PEOPLE ON A MISSION: SHARK SCIENTISTS

Aquariums and marine parks are often educational facilities too, in which scientists study sharks. Watching sharks in controlled environments helps researchers learn more about the animals. They can find out about their bodies and behavior. By learning about shark bodies and how they work, and better understanding shark behavior, scientists can share that information with conservationists. The conservationists can then put in place more measures to protect the animals in the wild.

Some shark research centers are set up with breeding programs for certain species of shark that are especially endangered in the wild. By breeding more of these types of sharks, people can help increase their numbers and provide a safety net that could prevent their extinction. If the animals were to die out in the wild, at least there would still be a population of captive sharks. One day, some of them could be released into the wild in the hope that they would breed there and a wild population of the sharks would grow once more.

Aquarium and marine parks often have veterinarians and veterinary facilities. If injured or sick sharks rescued in the wild are bought to the facilities, they can be treated and cared for.

SHARK RELATIVES IN DANGER

Several relatives of the shark are also in danger. Like the shark, they face threats to their populations and habitats, often due to human activities.

THE RAY

Rays are closely related to sharks. Like sharks, they are in danger from overfishing. Rays are hunted for their meat, fins, and other body parts. They are also victims of bycatch. Rays live in many of the habitats occupied by sharks, and their homes are also endangered due to pollution, coastal building activity, and tourism.

THE SKATE

Skates are close relatives of sharks and rays. They live in coastal waters, estuaries, and out in the ocean. Skates are often accidentally caught by fishermen when they use nets to trawl the seabed, where skates are usually found. That has caused damage to the population of these creatures. They too are affected by other threats including damage to their habitats.

THE CHIMAERA

Also known as the ghost shark or ratfish, the chimaera is a more distant relative of the shark. They are called ghost sharks because they have a pretty spooky appearance! They have large, reflective eyes that seem ghostly when light is shone on them. They also have smooth, scaleless bodies and long, whiplike tails. That makes them ghostly-looking creatures. The chimaera is found in deep-sea waters around the world, except the Arctic and Antarctic Oceans. Like the shark, its habitat has been damaged by climate change, among other factors. It has also been overfished.

THE SAWFISH

Sawfish are large, flat-bodied fish that have a long snout lined with teeth. It looks a little like a saw, which is how the animal got its name. Sawfish are one of the most threatened fish on Earth. They are listed as endangered or critically endangered on the IUCN Red List. The fish face threats to their survival due to overfishing for their fins, snout, and meat.

WHAT'S NEXT FOR THE SHARK?

Despite the efforts that are in place to try and help sharks, the future of endangered sharks is uncertain. Sharks are still overfished. Their habitat is being damaged and destroyed. Climate change is a growing threat, and sharks are still being sold in the illegal wildlife trade. More needs to be done if we are to protect these amazing animals and make sure sharks survive on Earth for many more millions of years.

REASONS TO BE HOPEFUL

The threat to sharks is very real. However, there is also good news for sharks. In some places, shark numbers are on the rise again. The success stories around the world include that of the great white shark in the Atlantic Ocean. There, these sharks are showing signs of population recovery thanks to bans on fishing. In Australia too, large marine parks are helping sharks such as the gray nurse shark and whale shark survive.

HELP FROM ORGANIZATIONS

Around the world, many organizations are taking action to help protect sharks. Oceana is the largest international organization focused on protecting Earth's oceans. It fights for endangered animals, including the shark, and carries out many research programs. Pew Charitable Trusts' Global Shark Conservation Campaign is designed to help end overfishing and protect shark populations around the world. These are just some of the many organizations that are helping people to learn and care about the amazing shark.

"Conservation efforts must focus on protecting both sharks and their habitats."

Dr Alison Kock, marine biologist and shark expert

Kids on a Mission

@mason_sharkSOS

When I grow up, I'm going to become a marine biologist. I want to study sharks in the wild and find out more about them. I love sharks. They are amazing.

HELP FROM ALL OF US

There is a huge amount that ordinary people everywhere can do to help sharks, too. We can all increase our efforts to live sustainably. That will help reduce the threat of climate change. We can raise awareness about the threat of the illegal wildlife trade. We can educate others about sharks and why we should help them. And we can make the most of events such as Shark Week, during which the magnificent shark is celebrated. Together, we can save the shark. And if we do that, these awe-inspiring predators will rule the oceans for millions of years to come.

MAKE IT YOUR MISSION: A CAREER IN CONSERVATION

Why not make it your mission to build a future career in conservation? That way, you could make a huge difference to sharks and other endangered animals. On pages 44–45 you'll find some of the conservation careers you could pursue. Below are ideas for things you can do right now to prepare for a career in conservation and help save sharks.

GET SET TO STUDY

Working hard at school now will pay off if you want a conservation career. Pay attention in your science, English, and geography classes. Languages are also useful. If you have a job overseas, being able to speak a foreign language is helpful.

GET CONNECTED

Connecting with other people who care about wildlife is a great way to feel empowered about saving endangered animals. You'll find some of the organizations you can join on page 47. By connecting with other people who are concerned about the environment, you'll find out what you can do to help. Being involved with conservation organizations and charities now will also help you when you apply for jobs in the future. It will show that you have been interested in conservation from an early age.

▼ By adopting a shark you'll be helping to conserve this beautiful species.

GET EXPERIENCE

Any form of work experience in wildlife care will be useful for a future conservation career. Why not apply to local zoos, charities, and conservation organizations as soon as you are old enough?

TAKE ACTION!

You'll have learned about some of the actions that help sharks from the Kids on a Mission features in this book. Here are some more ideas for other activities that can help protect sharks:

- Adopt a shark! Ask your parents to help you check out the World Wildlife Fund for Nature (WWF) or Shark Angels sites for information about adopting sharks.
- Bring your own reusable shopping bags to stores when you shop to help stop plastic entering the oceans. Recycle as much as you can—never throw away plastic (or other garbage).
- Join beach cleanup operations. The cleaner we keep our beaches, the less trash there will be in the oceans. We all need to play our part in keeping our oceans cleaner and healthier.
- Educate yourself and others about sharks. Watch good-quality television shows about sharks, and read great books about them, like this one! Tell your family and friends about what you have learned and encourage them to find out more. The better informed people are about sharks, the more they'll want to help them.
- Ask your school to hold a fundraising event to raise money for an organization such as Shark Angels, to help them protect sharks.
- Start a blog about sharks and the dangers they face. Educate as many people as you can.

◀ Taking part in a beach cleanup will help stop plastics and other garbage entering the oceans and harming wildlife there.

CAREERS IN CONSERVATION

Conservation is a huge growth area today, as more and more people turn their focus to concerns about the environment. There are a huge number of conservation jobs available. Here is information about just some of them—you can find out more about other conservation jobs by following the links on page 47 of this book.

▲ By working as a marine biologist you'll have a chance to observe ocean animals in their natural setting.

MARINE CONSERVATION BIOLOGIST

If you love the idea of working with ocean animals, you could become a marine conservation biologist. In this role, you would check on the health and wellbeing of animals in a natural area. You would also take care of the animals' habitat. You would help develop conservation strategies and plans to protect sharks and other marine animals in their habitats. A degree in environmental studies is usually needed.

WILDLIFE TECHNICIAN

Wildlife technicians study wildlife in its natural habitat. In this role, you would closely watch animal numbers and animal behavior. You could work for resource companies, environmental firms, and governments. You would help ensure that wildlife protection laws are followed. A degree in wildlife management is usually required.

MARINE ZOOLOGIST

Becoming a marine zoologist is a great step to take to help protect ocean animals. In this job, you would study ocean animal bodies and how the animals behave. You could work for marine parks, universities, governments, and also research organizations. Many zoologists travel for their work, to study many different animals in their natural environments. A biology degree is needed for this role.

PUBLIC EDUCATION AND OUTREACH SPECIALIST

In this role, you would teach people about wildlife such as sharks, and their habitats. That would include people in areas far away from the habitats, and people who live nearby. Giving talks to schools, to educate children about the importance of protecting wildlife, would also be part of your job. You might also give talks to people in organizations. That could include companies interested in helping wildlife. A degree in environmental studies is needed for this crucial job.

PUBLIC RELATIONS OFFICER

If you like raising awareness about important issues, this could be the role for you. Public relations officers manage communications between organizations and the public. In this job, you could work for charities, wildlife organizations, and governments. You would help run campaigns to make people aware of wildlife issues. A degree in marketing is useful.

JOBS IN ENVIRONMENTAL SCIENCE

There are many different roles in environmental science. For example, you could be a **climatologist** or a conservation scientist. A degree in environmental science is usually required for these jobs. If you want to become an environmental lawyer, you will need a law degree, with a specialization in environmental law.

If you love marine wildlife and are interested in a career in television or film, being an underwater camera operator could be your dream job. ▶

GLOSSARY

adaptable able to easily change to deal with new conditions
algae plantlike organisms that grow in damp places
aquarium a building that contains tanks of live fish and other ocean species
atmosphere the blanket of gases that surrounds Earth
bladder a body part that stores urine before it is excreted, or pushed out of the body
breed to mate to produce offspring
bycatch fish and other marine animals that are accidentally caught in fishing nets
camouflaged hidden against a natural background
carbon dioxide (CO2) a gas that contributes to climate change when released into the atmosphere
climate change a shift in the average weather conditions on Earth
climatologist a scientist who studies Earth's climate
conservation the protection of the planet
conservationists people who try and protect the planet
critically endangered facing an extremely high risk of extinction in the wild
endangered facing a very high risk of extinction in the wild
environments natural places where plants and animals live
estuaries areas where freshwater rivers meet salty oceans
extinction dying out
fins triangular-shaped body parts of a fish that help it maneuver in the water
fossil fuels fuels formed from the remains of plants and animals that lived long ago
geological related to Earth's structure
gills organs through which water flows and oxygen in the water is taken out
habitats places where plants and animals live
hatch to break out of a shell or casing
inhumane extremely cruel human behavior
lagoons areas of salt water that are separated from an ocean or a sea
mammals warm-blooded animals that feed their young with milk from their bodies
mangrove a tree or shrub that grows in tropical coastal areas
marine related to seas and oceans
marine biologist a scientist who studies the bodies and behavior of animals that live in seas and oceans
metabolism all the reactions that take place in an organism's body and use energy in the process
overgrazed describes an area of plants in which too many of them have been eaten
plankton tiny organisms that live in rivers and oceans and are eaten by some of the animals that also live there
pollution substances that are harmful to living things
populations all of the organisms belonging to one species and living in one place
porpoise a small, toothed whale
predators animals that hunt and eat other animals
preserving keeping safe
prey animals that are hunted and eaten by other animals
restoring making whole or healthy again
scales small, overlapping bony plates on a fish
senses the five senses of sight, hearing, smell, touch, and taste
species a type of plant or animal
sustainable describes something that is not harmful or that can be relied upon for the foreseeable future
territory an area that humans or other animals regard as their own
tourism the organization of vacations or trips to places in exchange for money
uterus part of a female animal's body in which a baby or babies grow

FIND OUT MORE

BOOKS

DK. *Shark* (DK Eyewitness). DK Children, 2022.

Eason, Katherine. *Sharks* (Food Chain Kings). Cheriton Children's Books, 2023.

Hestermann, Bethanie and Josh. *The Fascinating Ocean Book for Kids; 500 Incredible Facts!* (Fascinating Facts). Rockridge Press, 2021.

WEBSITES

Discover more about careers that help fight climate change at:
www.bestcolleges.com/blog/climate-change-jobs

Hear directly from people working in conservation! Find out what they have to say about working in a career in conservation at:
www.conservation-careers.com/conservation-jobs-careers-advice/how-to-get-a-job-in-conservation

Discover the ultimate guide to careers in conservation at:
www.conservation-careers.com/15-key-conservation-jobs-ultimate-guide-for-conservation-job-seekers

Discover careers in environmental science at:
https://jobs.environmentalscience.org

Find out more about the National Oceanic and Atmospheric Administration's (NOAA's) mission to champion shark conservation at:
www.fisheries.noaa.gov/international-affairs/shark-conservation

Discover more about shark and ray conservation at the WWF site:
https://sharks.panda.org

Publisher's note to educators and parents:
All the websites featured above have been carefully reviewed to ensure that they are suitable for students. However, many websites change often, and we cannot guarantee that a site's future contents will continue to meet our high standards of educational value. Please be advised that students should be closely monitored whenever they access the Internet.

INDEX

ABOUT THE AUTHOR

Sarah Eason has written a number of books on animals and the dangers they face. In researching this book, she has learned how magnificent sharks are and why everyone should try and help save them.